Nothing more is needed

on caring for our animals (and ourselves)

Christine King

Published by Dr. Christine King

Anima Books

Issaquah, WA 98027

animavet.com

ISBN: 0-9674926-3-7
ISBN-13: 978-0-9674926-3-6

Foreword

This book is as much a series of "Notes to Self" as it is a guide for anyone else. I forget or ignore these little gems and need to remind myself of them almost daily. In fact, that may be our biggest struggle as modern humans: to get over our clever, sophisticated selves and act simply as nature designed us, as an interwoven and inseparable part of all life. That might just be my most important Note to Self.

If you think this book reads a little like the Tao, you're right. The Tao is the inspiration not just for the style of this book, but also for its substance. Taking care of our animals (and ourselves) is, at its core, very simple. While much more *may* be said about caring for our animals and ourselves, how much more *need* be said?

To quote one of my favorite passages from the Tao:

> "Some say that my teaching is nonsense.
> Others call it lofty but impractical.
> But to those who have looked inside themselves,
> This nonsense makes perfect sense.
> And to those who put it into practice,
> This loftiness has roots that go deep.
>
> I have just three things to teach:
> Simplicity, patience, compassion.
> These three are your greatest treasures."

[translation by Stephen Mitchell]

Fundamentals

Food

i
Food is fundamental.
We eat to live.
We eat to fuel our lives
And take care of our bodies.

What we eat matters, because
What we eat becomes us.
It becomes our matter.

So, what we eat either enlivens us
Or it endeadens us.
Our choice.

ii
Feed every animal according to his nature:
Herbivores eat plants;
Carnivores eat animals;
Omnivores eat everyone.
(And everyone is eventually eaten.)

Grazers graze, browsers browse,
Hunters hunt, and scavengers scavenge.
Many animals roam or migrate for food.
To the best of your ability,
Feed every animal according to his nature.

iii
Feed every animal according to her needs:
The fat ones need less;
The thin ones need more;

Those feeding or working for others
Need also to eat for the other.

iv
Feed what nature has provided,
Just as nature has provided it:
Varied, fresh, full of life — and enlivening.

Food that is dried, cooked, refined —
Processed to death! —
Can make us feel heavy and dull.
It takes from us more than it gives,
So best to eat little of it.

v
Overeating likewise
Robs the body of vitality,
Both now and later.

Eat when you're hungry,
Stop when you're full.

Take what you need,
And leave the rest.

Take good care of our food supply,
And it will take good care of us.

As a great sage once said,
"Don't play with your food
Unless you've eaten all your toys."

Water

Water is essential.
Ah, but not all water sustains life.

Just like air, water is impartial;
It can also carry death. Toxic substances,
Microbes that don't belong on us or in us,
Disinfectants, other "public health" additives —
Invisible messages that do not sustain life.

To sustain life, water must be
Fresh, clean, alive,
Resonant with life — its own life.

Living water moves
In streams and springs,
In rain, in dew, and in plants.
This is the water that sustains life.

Where it came from determines its effect.
So, filter municipal water,
Filter polluted rain and well water.

Enliven still water by moving it.
Get it to swirl and flow,
Burble and dance.

Eat lots of plants, fresh, with
Their living water still in them.
Or if you're a carnivore,
Eat lots of animals who eat lots of plants,
Fresh, with their living water still in them.

Drink when you're thirsty,
Stop when you're full.

Take what you need,
And leave the rest.

Take good care of our water
And it will take good care of us.

Air

i
Fresh air is vital.
Breathe it in, with no other goal
Than to let the body breathe itself.

You cannot breathe for it.
"Breathing exercises": One more way
For the mind to tyrannize the body.

Instead, let go.
Let the body breathe for itself.
It knows how perfectly.

ii
Breathe fresh, clean air.
Air that is windswept,
Filtered through trees —
Created by trees! —
Refreshed by the elements.

Polluted air is dense and dull.
It makes us feel dense and dull.
It robs the body of vitality by
Burdening us with its garbage.

iii
Hidden dangers in the air we breathe
Cause alarm bells to ring in our bodies.
Sometimes in distressing ways.
Sometimes in less urgent ways,
But always in some way.

The least among us are often
The most affected.
They are our canaries in the coal mine.
We ignore their warning at our own peril.

To the best of your ability,
Provide fresh, clean air,
Air that has been moving through
And filtered by the whole of nature.

Allergies, you say?
That is not about the air,
But about the body.
Otherwise we'd all be sick.
To blame the air is to miss the point,
And miss the prompting to get well.

iv
Take good care of the air we breathe,
And it will take good care of us.

Drive less, walk more.
It'll do us all good.

So says my dog.
(Amazing how she knows best.)

Sunlight

i

Sunlight is water's mate.
We need both to live.
Yet too much or too little of either,
And we die.

ii

You cannot get sunlight out of a pill bottle
Or replicate it fully with a lamp.
Man has not yet trapped sunlight in a bottle
Or made it with a lamp.
And he never will.
Why would he even want to try?

Nature has placed the sun in the sky,
For all to enjoy for most of the year.
Even here, even in this rainy land
So far from the equator.

Nature has made of our skin and our eyes
Solar panels so that we may absorb
All the sunlight we need to be well.

And nature has made in us fat deposits
In which to store this precious vitamin "S."
All we need do is avail ourselves of some
Sunlight every day.

iii

And nature has stored sunlight in plants.
Unlike the alchemists, who vainly tried

And failed to convert lead into gold,
Plants convert sunlight into food
For all of us. Every day.

So, eat lots of leafy plants, especially green ones,
Every day.
Or if you are a carnivore,
Eat lots of animals who eat lots of plants,
Every day.

iv
Get outside every day.
Eat lots of plants every day.
That's how to get enough sunlight.

Cycles

i
Follow the cycles of the earth.
Even in climates whose seasons number only two,
Follow the rhythm of the year.

ii
Follow the cycles of the sun.
Get up when it's light,
Go to sleep when it's dark.
(Unless you are nocturnal,
In which case, do the opposite.)

Yes, in winter, you'll do less.
In summer, you'll do more.
So does nature.

iii
Follow the cycles of the moon.
Although they are less obvious
Than those of the sun,
The moon's cycles influence our bodies
Like nothing else.

Plants follow the cycles of the moon
Just as surely as they follow those of the sun.
When planting, tending, harvesting, and eating,
Follow the cycles of the moon.

If you don't know what the are,
Find out. Know the moon as well as the sun.

iv

Follow the cycles of the seasons.
Eat what nature has provided,
Fresh, and in season.

Seasonal foods are best.
The most fresh, the most tasty,
And the most wholesome.

Seasonal foods also help keep our bodies
In rhythm with the earth
And with the heavenly bodies that surround us.

Not just distant, disinterested neighbors,
The other heavenly bodies are like organelles
In this "single cell" of our shared universe.

Move in time with the rhythms of the earth.
Let the rhythms of the earth
And our heavenly neighbors
Move you.

v

Move with grace and ease
With the biggest rhythm of all:
Birth — Life — Death — Birth.
Just another cycle.

Rest

To replenish itself
And stay healthy,
The body needs rest.

Without good rest,
We break down
And eventually wear out.

To be good rest —
To be truly restful —
Rest requires comfort,
Peace and quiet,
And a sense of safety.

So, to the best of your ability,
Provide a comfortable, quiet,
Safe place for your animals to
Rest each day and
Sleep each night.

Rest when you're tired,
Get up when you're done.

Forget about what time it is!
Rest/sleep/nap when you need it.
My dog taught me this.
(Amazing how she knows best.)

Work

i

Intelligent life needs work.
Ah, but not toil or drudgery.
That's not work; it's slavery,
Working for someone else's benefit alone.

Intelligent life thrives
On work that is engaging,
Work that is a joy.

To be a joy, work must be appropriate,
Work must be productive,
And work must be rewarding.

When work is a joy, life is a joy.
When work is tedious or troublesome,
So is life.

Boredom is destructive to intelligent life.
The intelligence of life must be put to good use.
Self-sustaining and creative use.

ii

What work do wild animals do?

They feed themselves,
House and otherwise protect themselves,
Raise their young, and adapt their surroundings
To better suit them.

It is not tedious work, nor troublesome.
Nor boring.
And it is not all-consuming, as we shall see.
It is life itself, taking good care of itself.

iii
Take care to avoid work that is excessive,
Exhausting, or injurious.
There is no wisdom in "No pain, no gain."
No wisdom at all. And no truth.

To the best of your ability,
Provide work that your animals enjoy.
And provide opportunities for your animals
To take good care of themselves.
For that is good work.

Play

i
Play is as essential to life
As work.

In fact, play may be fundamentally
What life is all about, what life is up to.
Why else all the exuberant variety,
All the splendid silliness?

ii
Work that is playful is blessed.
Play that is productive is blessed.
But play that is purposeless
Is divine.

Its purpose is in its purposelessness,
Its pointlessness, its end unto itself.
Its purpose is in its lightness, its freedom,
For therein is its life.

iii
Do wild animals play?
Need you even ask?

Consider the otter,
Idling down the stream on his back,
His furry little tummy soaking up the sun.

Consider the hawk,
Wings outstretched, paragliding
Lazily on a thermal updraft and gazing for miles.

Consider the fox cubs
Playing dungeons and dragons
While their mother looks on, kind, indulgent, smiling.
Need I go on?

iv

Play often. And to the best of your ability,
Provide your animals with plenty of opportunities
For play. Silly, pointless, purposeless play.
For therein one savors the essence of life.

My dog and her friends taught me this, the
Essentiality of play, and how to throw oneself
Wholeheartedly into play, as if
Our very lives depend upon it.

Oh, the sorrowful expression on her face
When I say I don't have time for play today.
I think she feels very sorry for me at these times.
I think she may be right.
(Amazing how she knows best.)

Love

i
Loving social bonds are as essential
As food, water, air, sunlight, seasons...
We need each other in order to be well.

ii
Oh, but not the gooey sentimentality
That so often passes for love.

Love is robust and resilient,
Strong, without needing to grasp or cling,
And brave enough to be selfless.

Not the fake "selflessness" of
Emotional martyrdom, emotional blackmail,
But a dissolving of the boundaries of separate self;
Me and you dissolved into WE.

Thus, love is not a sentiment,
It is an experience.
Of life.
It's how life is to be lived.

iii
Loving social bonds are essential.
Good company makes us feel good,
And it makes us feel safe.

Even science has proven the importance
Of loving and being loved.

Why do anything we don't love?
Why be anywhere we don't love?
Why be with anyone we don't love?

Heaven and hell are here and now:
Heaven is found with those we love.

iv
But while loving social bonds
Surely do cross species divides,
There is simply no substitute
For being with one's own kind.

There is nothing like the instant
Understanding and acceptance
Of one's own kind.
Ah, to be truly understood: heaven.

So, make sure dogs have dog friends,
Horses have horse friends,
Chickens have chicken friends — and
Humans have human friends.

To make my dog be my best friend
Is to disrespect and disregard her dogness.
And my humanness.

v
To the best of your ability,
Treat the social bonds your animals make
As just as precious as your own.
Because to love and be loved: heaven.
My dog taught me this.

Death

And so we come now to death.

i
Death comes to us all.
It is nothing to be feared,
Nothing to be resisted.
As if it could be resisted. Ha!
Here, if anywhere, "resistance is futile."

Death — and dying — is not complicated.
Neither is it a problem to be solved or an
Enemy to be fought against, pushed back
Until the last possible moment.
It is only we, who fear it so, who make it so.

Death is best accepted as one of the ways
Life transforms itself into something else.
Into what? Who can say.
Probably into another life, wouldn't you think?

ii
When the prospect of death —
One's own death or that of a beloved —
Is met with equanimity, one's
Life forever changes.
We can live without fear, without dreading loss.
And we can love without fear, without dreading loss.

A young dog with an inherited disease
Once told me this:
"We show you how to love without hanging on."

To love with the lightest possible touch,
With an open hand that is both
Free to receive
And to let go when the time comes.

With sadness, yes, but without
That dreaded sense of loss.
Because what we held so gently in our hand
Was never really ours
And is never really lost.

iii
Oh, to live like that every day!
Heaven.
Such is the gift of being
On friendly terms with death.

My dog has taught me this.

To love a dog or a cat or a horse or a human
Is to sign up for a master class in love and loss.
Like the monks who sleep in coffins to
Inure themselves to the prospect of death,
Almost daily I imagine life without her.

How much sweeter it makes life with her!

Incidentals

Disease

Disease comes to us all
From time to time.
Yes, but why? Why!

Disease is how our bodies show us
That we have lost our way.

When disease appears, go back.
Go back to the beginning.
Find out where we have failed to
Follow the fundamentals.

Ah, but what of injury?
When injury appears, go back.
Go back to the beginning.
Find out where we have failed to
Follow the fundamentals.

Oh, but what of degeneration?
And of proliferations, of <gasp> cancer!
When these conditions appear, go back.
Go back to the beginning.
Find out where we have failed to
Follow the fundamentals.

Disease is how life shows us
That we have lost our way.

The good news is that it also shows us
The way back.

Movement

Movement is a characteristic of life.
Life moves.

Living things are always moving
In some way.
Some movements are huge,
Some are miniscule,
But living things are always moving.

To stop moving is to stagnate.
Stagnation is a prelude
To death.

So, to be fully alive, move!
Move every part.
Healthy and diseased.
Body. Mind. Emotions. All of us.

Rabbit Holes

My dear friend:
Before you disappear down that rabbit hole,
Take note of where you began,
And why.

Even if the journey changes inconceivably,
You will always find your way out again
If you only remember why you went down there
In the first place.

There are many, many twists and turns.
You may lose your way, lose heart,
Backtrack, and end up coming out
Exactly where you went in,
Empty-handed
And feeling like the journey was an utter waste.

But if you're brave, and you can leave
Your preconceived notions at the door,
You may very well find what it is
You're truly looking for.

Kinship

Be on friendly terms with all life.

You don't have to like
Every one of your relatives.

But it is wisdom itself to
Recognize our inseparable
Kinship with all life.

Selfishness

Life is selfish.
And life is co-operative.
In equal measure.

Appreciate both, for both are
Essential qualities of life.

Focus on one, and you'll
Fail to see the other.

The wholly "selfless" one neglects
To take care of its self,
And so suffers from neglect.

The wholly "selfish" one neglects
To take care of others,
And so suffers from isolation,
Division, divisiveness, and thus
Perpetual war against others.

Practice selfishness and co-operation
In equal measure, for both are
Essential qualities of life.

Peaceful co-existence and co-operative action.
Autonomy within community.
A community of whole individuals,
Free to co-operate with, and care for, one another.

Strife

Why strife?
See *Selfishness*.

Omissions

What about all else we've come to consider
Fundamental to animal care?

Vaccination, deworming, dental care,
Supplements, saddle fit, hoof care...

Yes, there is a time and a place
For all of them.

But the interesting thing is that
When we live as nature designed us
And designed for us,
It's amazing how much of life
Takes care of itself.

Communication

To be understood,
First understand.

As another great sage once said,
"It is more important to understand
Than to be understood."

To understand another,
Put yourself in her place.

Merge with the other, then
See what she sees, hear what she hears,
Feel what she feels.

Then you will understand;
And in understanding,
Be understood.
Because the two are now one.

Parasites

i
Why parasites?

Parasites are life feeding on itself.
Just as herbivores eat plants,
Carnivores eat animals,
Omnivores eat everyone,
And everyone is eventually eaten.

So, around and around we go.
No matter where you begin,
The cycle completes itself.

ii
Parasites have a place and a purpose.
Their place is on or in another.

Does that make us parasites of the earth?

Just as "weeds" are plants that are growing
Where we don't want them or that
We haven't found a use for,
"Parasite" is our label for those who are living
Where we don't want them or that
We haven't found a use for.

But life is far more interesting than that!

And as we are beginning to discover,
Parasites do indeed have a purpose.
Probably several.

What if "parasites" are
Symbionts in disguise, and simply
Out of place or out of balance?

Symbiosis: together we all flourish.
Apart, we all struggle.

iii
How do "parasites" help us flourish?
They show us where we are weak,
And in so doing, they stimulate us
To become strong
Or to bow out and start over.
Which is another way of becoming strong.

They show us where we are ineffective,
And in so doing, make us more effective.
They can even help calm our self-destructive
Hypervigilance by redirecting our attention
Back to what's most important: *balance.*

They share our resources,
And we share theirs, which include
A breathtaking resilience and adaptability.
Life itself, irrepressible and everlasting
In one form or another. Cohabiting. Coexisting.
Peacefully? That all depends on us.

Thus, they speak of balance.
Its lack, our need, for balance.
They help bring us back into balance,
Both with our own "parasites" and with
Our own unwitting parasitism.

So, "parasites": *Symbionts* out of place
Or out of balance with the whole.
No matter the species.

iv

"Oh, but don't parasites cause disease?
Shouldn't we therefore do something about them?"

Certainly. But what?
Parasitism is the symptom, not the disease.

What if, rather than nuking all the parasites,
We feed the host, nourish and
Strengthen the host, and thereby
Restore a healthy balance between
The host and its symbionts.

My dog is terribly sensitive to fleas.
Do I kill them?
Yes, regrettably I do.
And every time I ask myself:
Is that short-term gain worth the long-term loss?

At what cost do we destroy parasites
Without first understanding
Their place and their purpose?

Mightn't there be a better way?

Small Things

i
Life consists of big things and small things.
The big things are communities of small things,
Although we seldom see it that way.

Our bodies are communities of small things,
Microbes included. Our "silent partners,"
We need them, and they need us, for
"They" are "us." Bugs R us.

We are each a walking, talking ecosystem,
A big community of small things,
Not an "us" invaded by "them."

The fear and loathing leveled at microbes
Is fear and loathing of some of
Our very own processes!
For we are WE, not "they" and "us."

Be on friendly terms with your microbes.
Nourish them, cherish them,
And they will do the same for you.
Because we are a community. Practice
Peaceful coexistence and co-operative action.

ii
When we make an enemy of these "others,"
We create for ourselves a perpetual war,
A never-ending battle for survival
Of "us" against "them."
That's one way of operating.

But not a very good one,
Because in the process we may end up
Destroying ourselves.
MADness: Mutually Assured Destruction.

Oh, but what about Lyme disease, lepto,
E. coli, MRSA, flesh-eating bacteria...
All those horrible infections?!

Yes, some microbes do not belong on us or in us.
But many do. Cohabiting, coexisting.
Peacefully? That all depends on us.

When any living thing finds itself in a
Hostile environment, it fights for its life.
So, whose fault is it — if blame be needed —
When a microbe finds itself
Unwelcome on us or in us?

What if Pasteur was onto something
In his deathbed concession:
"The microbe is nothing; the terrain is everything."
What if we were to act from this perspective?

Must we make such a fuss? Why not just
Quietly usher out those that don't belong
And make a place for those that do.

What if, rather than "killing the invaders,"
We feed the host, nourish and
Strengthen the host, and thereby
Restore a healthy balance between
Big thing and small things.

iv

Oh, but what of viruses?
Surely there is nothing good about a virus?

Consider this:
Each virus is little more than code,
Small packets of DNA or RNA.
Information. Succinct bits of genetic code.
Remarkably like our own...

Consider, too:
Most viruses are species-specific.
And with those that aren't, their effects are
Essentially the same in all of us.
After all, we have so much in common.

So, might viruses be small fragments of ourselves,
Separated at some time of distress or disintegration,
Trying to find their way home through whatever
"Chinks in our armor" they can find?

Might they even be one way that life evolves?
Information, shared.
Viruses: wayfarers, sharing news, offering views
We might otherwise not have seen.

What if we were to view viruses not as our enemies,
But as part of ourselves? As belonging.
Inviting them back home, might that not help to
Heal us all?

Balance

Live, and let live.

Take what you need and leave the rest.
This way, we all get what we need.

Eat when you're hungry,
Drink when you're thirsty,
Rest when you're tired...
And stop when you're replenished.

Take what you need; it's there for you.
But leave what you don't need; it's there for others.

This way, we all get what we need.
We never take too much,
And we never leave others in need.

About the Author

Christine King is an Australian veterinarian who
has been following wherever her interest has taken
her ever since graduating from vet school in 1985.
It has led her through rural and equine practice,
residencies in equine medicine at leading veterinary
teaching hospitals in Australia and the US, a Master's
degree in equine exercise physiology, veterinary
research, veterinary publishing — and about a decade
ago into the realm of herbal medicine and other forms
of complementary and alternative medicine.

She now lives in the Seattle area with her beloved dog,
The Splendid Miss Tiger Lilly.

www.ingramcontent.com/pod-product-compliance
Lightning Source LLC
Chambersburg PA
CBHW071448040426
42445CB00012BA/1480